MORMON
BOY

Cover Art: Glenn Brown, "Shallow Deaths" 2000

Author Photograph: Olivia Tucker

Cover and Book Design: Joel A. Bass

ISBN: 978-1-932-418-43-9

Elixir Press
PO Box 27029
Denver, Colorado 80227

www.ElixirPress.com

Library of Congress Cataloging-in-Publication Data

Tucker, S. Brady.
Mormon boy / S. Brady Tucker.
p. cm.
ISBN 978-1-932418-43-9 (alk. paper)
I. Title.
PS3620.U328M67 2012
811'.6--dc23
2011036277

Elixir Press is a nonprofit literary organization.

MORMON BOY

SETH BRADY TUCKER

[signature]

Litfest
2012

As always, for Olivia

Contents

IV: The Best Man In All The World

I. Falling in Love During Wartime

The Road to Baghdad

Is less a road than a floral
collection of spongy and soft
bodies, a gathering of the myriad

colors of nations—burnt umber,
puce, kiln red, olive drab, hot
steel. It is a road that stretches

eternally into the ochre mocha
of the horizon. The road
to Baghdad has its own atmosphere

and sound, so unlike the roads
I have driven in the States—here,
the road is silent but for the pops

and spits of flame where trucks
clutch the bright and colorful
bodies of the unfortunate dead.

The road to Baghdad is like the aftermath
of a Fourth of July parade—streets
littered with the chaos of celebration,

where dyed paper and the bright
hulls of fireworks gather in the gutter.
Sometimes, I look for the road

to Baghdad in old maps or on
the web, but I can never find
it—the distance of time has cleared

it from the record books, has erased
it from everywhere but my mind, and
from the minds of those soldiers who saw

it with me. Today, I awake in the morning
with unexplained scratches on the bridge
of my nose, and I ask my empty room, where

has that road gone? I understand that if there
is no road, then there is no me. But if none
of this ever really happened, how do I awaken

every morning to the sun burning my outline
into the wild asphalt of that beautiful highway?

Falling In Love During Wartime

I am missing eleven months, nine days, and give or take, fourteen minutes from my life.
A good portion of 1990 is lost, and a large piece of 1991 has disappeared. People talk

to me about Brokaw's War Time America as if I were there, as if these pieces of someone
else's life could exist. I missed the yellow-ribbon orgy, the flags flying for "the boys

over there," the night when everyone closed together around their radios and televisions
ready to mourn the fallen, or exult for their heroes. The robbery was complete and crimson,

it was ancient, it was cleansing, it was eternal. I'm sure that the beaches in North Carolina
were quiet that year; the water was warm, the sand on the beach yielding, and the girls too—

worried for strangers like only beautiful, uninvolved people can be. Here is what I want:
I want that night, that night when I am twenty-one, when I can buy alcohol legally,

when I can sit in the dark night of the park with the girl I should be in love with. I know her
because she existed for me in the desert, at night rising with the cold roasted moon. She

is fair and olive skinned, her hair a light brown, and she is thin and muscular as a fawn.
It is no secret that she comes from the only pornography we had in the gulf: the Victoria's

Secret Fall issue, which I still own. And she understands me like only I understand
me, and we are leaving the party on campus, we are holding hands like people hold hands

when holding hands is new to them--anxiously, moistly, tightly. We are leaving the party
because we cannot bear to watch this war that is on television. Maybe we are too sensitive

to violence, or maybe we just don't want to be reminded that there are people just like us
in a desert that has turned cold and hungry and mean, a desert that is trying to swallow up

everything above it, and we don't want that on our conscience, we don't want to think
of men walking into white flashes of light, into red tracer rounds, into the blackest

fortress of sound imaginable, into faces streaked with tears, into faces streaked with blood
and tears, into faces streaking in front of their vision, soldier fingers tightening around triggers

uncertainly even though those fingers, those hands, have been trained to obey, and these
boys, who are as handsome as they will ever be, wonder if the bullets hitting their chests

will feel like paper cuts or like explosions, if it will be clean or if it will be messy. We
walk out of that party, in love, our eyes linking like bodies copulating, and the bottle

of wine is in my hand. We are both feeling high—we are six beers and a half bottle
of Boone's Farm Strawberry Hill into it, drinking while we watch faceless soldiers

push up on an invisible border that is already in flames above the skyline. We had
to leave, our feelings for those soldiers impelling us to rise and escape with our wondrous

love intact. We walk to the park. It is cool out, the grass is cold where the dew
has touched, yet the earth still harbors the heat of the day underneath. We are barefoot

and the streets are empty. The static sound of gunfire is far off, pouring from the blue
flickering lights of the houses, and we are walking away, letting the sound fade

until only our breath can be heard, swallowed up by the simple sounds of our sweet
and innocent blood moving through muscle and bone. We sit on a peeling park

bench, I wipe the wet night off before she sits, and we move close—the heat of our bodies
swirls with the cool night as we move, and we drink wine from the bottle and she has

a glistening shade of pink wine above her lip for a split second before she licks it off.
And the look in her eyes right then—like there is a metaphor for that. The darkness

is swallowing us, it is closing around us, pulling the light from the stars away, and the moon,
and there is only reflected light to see by, and her face is pale and sharp, as if the dark

has outlined her face in pastels, and all I can think about is how lucky I am to be this guy,
here with her, and the night agrees; the night takes us and lets the alcohol do its work.

We embrace, and I can feel the soft ripple of her ribcage against mine, and I can feel
the side of her breast with my arm, and her breath is moist against my ear as she whispers

things about love past our long hair, which is entwined like the dark grass of the park.
She tells me she will never leave me alone, that we will be together forever,

and I know she is lying, but it feels so good to hear it that I will believe it eternally.
Tomorrow will be the same. We will come to this park again. I will feel like the world

is collapsing into itself, that I could reach out through the walls and soothe the loneliness
of Mr. Earnest next door, that I am a part of it all, that I will feel how it feels to be a part

of Blitzer's *America At War* from the outside, I will wake up with the dreams
of a civilian, I will hold a candle out on an all-night vigil, I will stand in protest

I will hang ribbons I will support our boys over there I will pray even though
there is no god I will remember things that never happened I will fill the space

between the boy on the bench and the boy in the desert and I will always, always, make sure he is with someone. I will maintain that the desert is a fiction, a fiction

of lights and noise, and I will assert to the boy on the park bench that he will never have to feel like he was a part of something missing, that the years would

be kind, that his sleep would wind like silk, and unlike the boy in the desert, when he looks up, the bright sun will shine upon his face without passing through.

Dead Man

I am a dead man. Dead
18 years. I laugh and dance
the cabbage patch and tell
jokes on myself, and I make up

lies and I drive an expensive SUV
and play basketball on Saturdays
and tivo *Survivor* and I fake
it all so that the people around

me will not be disappointed
that I did not make it home again,
because it makes their life so much
easier to believe that the war was just,

and they are proud to know a combat
veteran instead of some unlucky kid
who died because he was in the wrong
place at the wrong time for the wrong

reasons. I am a dead man. When
they find out the truth, they will trace it
back to February 22nd, 1991, Iraq,
the day I saw a man die on the road

to Baghdad, the day I helped to hide
him in a black body bag, the day I
helped to hide many others in black
body bags, but what did it matter

if I was already dead? Do you see?
How could it matter? Soon, they will
discover the truth, that I am a dead
man, lost, acting my way through life

until it all catches up with me.
I am a dead man, a dead man
dead 18 years, dead the 43rd day
of boot camp, when I helped hold

down an annoying farm boy from Idaho,
a boy we traumatized until Tree just
unexpectedly hit him with an entrenching
tool, and we scattered while he bled away,

but Tree could not hide, and was found
and locked away in Leavenworth,
and the boy from Idaho was finally
discharged, but was never the same

again, and I have heard that he is dead
like me, and locked in a black casket
in Idaho by family who thought he
was alive, and I have never lived a day

since that day in boot camp, and I think
about that boy from Idaho, and how it must
have killed him, to be bullied and harassed
again, just like in High School, and that

being a soldier was not enough, and therefore,
probably nothing would ever be enough, and
like brothers, I am a dead man, dead like
him, dead 18 years even though

people who know me will say that
they cannot believe that I have not
been alive this whole time, what with
the two useless degrees and my penchant

for drink, and they will not believe that it all
didn't happen in the desert, on a road
mirrored by a pipeline, because they
have heard my stories, and it is true

to an extent that I did some dying there,
but dying is not dead, and dead is how
things have been and will always be,
and dead is what I look like when

I open my eyes and am finally able to see.

And the Way the Sun Was Positioned

I thought you were smoking a cigarette—
just kicking back for the moment against
the warm metal of a deuce and a half
truck, in the shade. There were puddles
of oil running from underneath the truck,
leaking from bullet holes where rounds
had pierced the engine block. Your leg
was wet from one large ebony puddle, but
we were all dirty then, so it didn't seem to
matter.

Your M-16 was across your chest, and your
forearm was draped over the handgrip
in such a comfortable manner, I thought
for a moment you were asleep. So I just sat
down by your side. I hadn't eaten yet, so
I tore open an MRE, threw the sealed package
of *beef, dehydrated* away and began to
eat the peanut butter on the dry crackers.
You were looking back over the low ridge,
where smoke seemed to be oozing from the
pores of the earth in spurts. And I thought
that dying would be easy now, like sunshine
is easy, or hammocks. I thought that
after what we had seen and done that day
that everything after would be a piece of cake.

But I wasn't ready to go back, over that ridge
you were looking at, over to where bodies
held on to metal like scorpions hold onto
flying beetles. Back there, I wasn't ready
to go, and I was glad for you being there, and
I wanted to tell you so. I said, "Danny."
and you hitched like you were about to
vomit. And you turned and looked at me,
and I could see the cigarette in your hand,
how it was ashes down to the filter, and how
the oil (you said it, 'ole') didn't look so much
like oil anymore, and how your eyes seemed gray
with your skin, and all I wanted right then
was a burning cigarette so bad.

Regrets Number 191: The Bosnian

So, an old girlfriend (see poem *Regrets Number 82: Old Girlfriends Never Die*)
and I pick up these three foreign travelers (one girl from Holland, one boy

from Venezuela, one boy from Bosnia) and within a few minutes this crazy bitch
has invited them to stay with me for the week. We get to my tiny dank place

in the Haight and try to have a conversation in my den, which has us sitting almost
knee to knee, but it is splitting into like fifty directions (imagine the play by play

of the three languages: each fouling and double-dribbling and getting back-court
violations, and English is doing a terrible job at referee (this metaphor goes out

to Train Williams—a teammate of mine in college)). Then this conversation goes
ghetto on us, a real street-ball game with fouls and dunks and under-cutting because

we add absinthe and Crazy Horse malt liquor to the mix, and soon I am embellishing
my stories of the Persian Gulf War—trying to engender pity or get laid, I don't know,

and it is three years later that I realize what an ass I was, that the Bosnian must have felt
like he was missing something important in the translation of my history, because to him,

this poor American maniac is not seeing the critical difference between, A: putting
dead total fucking strangers into body bags, and B: loading your dead mother (shot in face)

and sister (raped and shot in liver) and mailman (land-mine) onto a mule drawn
cart headed to a landfill, because nobody has the energy to dig graves anymore.

Whirligig

The Dead:

When he is alone, in an
easy chair, say, or in the dark,
under a raspberry jam night sky, sitting
on his oak deck, he hears them:

he hears Sammy and Doug and Erik whisper
their jealousy—they whisper their hatred for
his life and the world simmers with a
heat terrible heat, and he is not

alone for a moment, but awfully
surrounded by them again, and he
knows what they mean when they
speak to him, and his blood red and blue

from heart to arteries to veins
beats like syrup and he is in the desert
again, his knee in the sand, his tan
desert combat boots dug in as if

rooted there, and he hears again the
sound of them whispering with the voices
of bullets popping and whirring and
thumping flesh, and he hears them

roar their fear so loud and awful
and terrible that his weapon falls to his
feet and his gloved hands hold bloody
chunks of sand against his ears

to drown out the sound of it all. When
it is over, he shakes the sand out of
his high and tight, and he picks up his
discarded weapon in shame. To the east, bombs

and bullets still purr as a war rends everything
he knows and every thing he ever will know.
When he is alone, they remind him:
"You will never be alone, bud. Never."

The Alive:

When there are other people around,
he knows that some of it isn't
real—like how the feel of Erik's
blood sticking to the black metal

of his weapon was real, or how the
oily smoke of Erik's blood burned his
nostrils when his weapon overheated was real.
Real real. And he knows this is wrong and untrue

and he is as afraid of getting help
as he was in that desert when everything
went wrong in the world. So he pretends
that they are not a fiction, that they exist,

like Erik's severed foot existed still tied
into its boot—how it felt to pick up that
foot and place it in a pile of other things that
were Erik's, and sometimes it even works for him.

Do you see why he thinks of the world like
proverbs in fortune cookies? "Burning flesh is
the smell of success!" or, "You are alive for some
obscure reason." He smiles sometimes when

he thinks like this, but he knows it isn't funny.
He knows that they will continue to whisper to
him for the rest of his life, and that he is doomed
and lost and cursed. No one will ever laugh with him

and no one will ever know the cowardice he is capable
of, and how Erik would be alive if it weren't for him.
But know this: somehow, one night, he will know five minutes
of peace—just five minutes of life, as it should have been.

The Cold Logic of Farm Animals

1. How To Lift a Wallet From a Dead Soldier

The Bedouins kept their distance, and I don't blame them.
We must have seemed like mechanical beasts: our glaring
metal eyes, our Kevlar chests and skulls, our boots crushing
one million years of human erosion. At night we would curse

the cold of the sand. It would bully us into our hard holes
in the ground, into sleeping-bags that let the freezing indifference
of the desert seep up into our aching bones. I know I went crazy
some nights. Someone has the video to prove it, but I should make sure

you understand: none of these things happened. During the day
we would curse the heat. We would curse the bloated bodies
tangled along the pipeline road. In the beginning we covered
our mouths with surgical masks and our hands with sanitized

rubber gloves. Jenkins said we were combat surgeons. We knew
it wasn't happening. The highway melted and sucked at our boots.
The tar melted like tongues. We walked like Boris Karloff
in a colorized horror show. We got used to the smell of the dead.

2. Our Dreams All Looked Exactly Like This

Mattress. Broken teeth. Need. Titties. Femur.
Some nights we would awake on the ground,
arms wrapped around one another for warmth,
and we would know our dreams were not

our own, that Jenkins was dreaming about
a pizza shop where a dead boy waits tables,
and the saliva is just oozing out at the thought
of a tomato and ham pizza, and the boy waits

on all the tables around Jenkins, offers him no help.
We knew that our dreams were different only in that
the pizzas had different toppings. Sausage and onion,
and the serving boy with a gaping hole in his heart.

3. *Company Matters*

We got used to the company of the dead.
We got used to every terrible and meaningless
dream. With every bowling ball sun rolling
lazily away, my fart sack would inch its way
to the piles of meat. The black zippered bags
looked so soft—like luxurious mattresses

set in a row. Steve Martin came to see us before
the war started, and he shook my hand, but wouldn't
look me in the eye. I thought for sure it was
an omen (we soldiers are a superstitious lot)—
that it meant I was going to get shot in the head
like JFK. Later, I found out he didn't look

at anyone, which was good because then maybe
that's what saved me. None of this is confirmed:
I got up at four in the morning. I drank one thousand
cups of coffee a day. No—that isn't true either. I drank
fifty cups of coffee a day. I held dead men in my arms.
I put them in zippered bags. They waved to me before

I pulled the tab up over their heads. Some held fingers
to their lips in order to quiet me. They were like lincoln
logs in their symmetry. I appreciated that. This
is confirmed: everything was just differing shades
of brown. I turned sopping wet copper with blood.
Some of the men were dry like fig trees. Some reminded

me of the kind Pakistani bus drivers who gave
me unleavened bread to eat on my birthday—
the first real food in a hundred days.
Some gifts grow on you.
Some gifts take everything from you.
Some leave you solitary and strange.

4. *Truth and Rumors*

Rumors: I cried once. The gift of unleavened bread from a Pakistani is a delicately savored
memory, which can only mean it was a dream. This dream is death soup. It is entitled,
"How to make Jesus a hat that fits," or, "The Zen master says, None of your fucking business."

There are one thousand... No... That would be a lie. There are fifteen people in the world who are
holding on to the greatest memories of their lives, and you are a major player in those memories.
And you have forgotten your part.

Truth: I cried once. I told a joke over the body of a man with no jaw and no arm and no right
eye and no feet and no ring finger and no ear and no pants because the pants were blown off
and the pants were clean but shredded a few yards away. I couldn't finish the joke even though
we had been doing this unconfirmed for thirty-three days fifteen hours forty minutes and
because of the smell and because his ring finger was missing and because it never happened
that way because there is no way these things can happen and the punch-line to the joke eight
years later: But they are twins--if you've seen Juan, you've seen Amal, could not have cleansed
the dry fig soul of any one of us.

5. Sleeping Through Murder

I wake up at my grandfather's house as if I slept on cold, iron concrete.
I wake to the gamy smell of feathers, to the barking of a chicken chasing dog,
to the scream of a rooster, to the last chaos of feathers, red, black, white,
one on top the other, piling in consilience, piling in one disconcerting sentiment.

The rain has stopped falling. Somewhere I hear the slap of a beaver tail on a lake,
the last icicle falling from the barn roof. In the corral the mud is watching me
from one thousand tiny bubbles disguised as black dilated pupils. On the porch,
one solitary drop of rusty blood. I know I am home, that is all over, but I also feel

I am being watched. Under our porches, someone is keeping score—how many
stubbed toes, how many slivers, how many bloody footprints on rough wooden
stairs, how many tons to a rain-cloud, questions like where do the blades of grass go
when they are lonely. In heaven, things are tallied on an ancient abacus. The porch

is a counterpoint, the porch takes no for an answer everyday, and cruelly, pitilessly,
I live in this awkward, solipsistic anticipation of death—hoping I will be able
to form brilliant last words. Will my epitaph be in the form of a question, or just
a silly apology? The question that I never ask: Why are there blood stains

on the old oak steps to my grandfather's house? You figure it out. The porch
will be keeping score. Feathers swirl like debris, filling the corner of the deck
like rounded off Arapahoe totems. A rooster squeals once then is content to wheeze
a pain so acute the sound of it is the color of blood, and the only thing worse

would be a horse on fire, or the garbled thrashing of a drowning elephant,
the hiss of lava cooking offal. From the musty corral a mule stands
trembling, confused by the weather, the swirl of feathers, the light reflecting
off the rusty bathtub in the nail room, the rubber waders I wear, my pale face.

Water leaks from the roof, slowly filling a water-trough. A dog barks. The sound
spills water over the lip of the trough, and the water tastes like regret mocking every
move. For all these things, I imagine that it is the absence of light that is most disturbing.
This life seems like a tax return to me, and I wonder at the soft crumbling and gray

porch of my grandfather's house, at the bloody footprints on warped boards, I wonder
if words of wisdom will suffice. If there was a god, he would tell me where they came
from, he would show me the cuts on the balls of their feet. Would this ever appease me?
On the porch, the calligraphy of blood answers no, no, no, always the contrarian.

6. *Artifacts of Scholarship*

We would watch the sun
roll like a ball toward
the twilight crease of
sky and earth.
We hoped it would
destroy everything
in its path. In the morning,
the same disappointments,
and the evening always
letting us down.

Telling you these things
will not help you.

Someone said only through
parable will wisdom come.
You will not share
this with your
friends. You will claim
these bloody stories
as your own.

Because none of
this could ever happen.

7. *Totems the Rooster Carves*

He likes disguises.
He enjoys the way
ice plays pavement,

the way the desert
is cool six inches
down.

He likes Wednesdays
because they feel
like Fridays.

Tonight, Jenkins
dreams he is
on the edge
of the Grand

Canyon—he
watches the sky
as it attaches itself
to the rusty bottom.

He walks to
the edge, for he
admires disguises.
The desert wind blows
down on him as
it enters the great chasm,
and he turns when he
imagines he feels
the hand of a lover on
his shoulder.

Only the oil fires
behind him
destroy
the illusion.

8. *The Dream of the Chicken Coop*

Corporal Jenkins is a child in his dreams, forever following his skinny twelve
year-old cousin, whose sharp sunburned features and avian nose seem purposefully
hidden by a greasy sweep of dirty blonde hair. His eyes are shiny blue, and peek
out from behind his hair like the naked light of a bulb through penitentiary windows.

The two of them wake to feed the chickens, his cousin filling up the morning
with streams of fine greenish brown tobacco, spit onto a dusty path where it rolls
into cloudy balls. He smiles a flat yellow grin, like boards lying in rot. His boots
suck in the black mud, he lumbers, he does not speak. His cousin opens the rusty

gate of the coop, scattering stupid and ugly chickens who wildly run for an exit
that doesn't exist. They calm, peck, stupidly strut, toes turned in and asses swinging,
starved because all they know is hunger. The chickens frighten Jenkins. The boys step
around the fowl, collect shovels from the sharp hooks on the wall. Jenkins can smell

hot clay and the sharp alkaline of urine. They bend to the work, straw and bird-shit
and soil mounding in the split dark of the coop. The chickens mill about their feet,

barely evading the blades of the shovels as they chunk hard into the ground. Sweat
drips from Jenkins' brow, darkens his faded and worn nightshirt. He digs harder,

faster, anxious to bring the work to an end, and his shovel blade bites into a cavernous
hole, comes up bloody like mad, chaotic sound. Then, the frenzy of chickens, wild
for the pink bodies wiggling in the uncovered mouse den. The chickens are clambering
over his feet to get at the blind, finger-length mice, and for a moment he uses his unlaced

boots to hold them at bay. His cousin looks on in wonder, happy for the distraction,
any distraction, from the work. One chicken swallows the oblivious and broken
bodies whole, gorging on the mice as they lay like kindling, jockeying for the best
position possible for their absent mother's nipples. His cousin watches like a dog under

a porch. His cousin can appreciate the uniformity of the dying. One dead mouse
flips over and onto a chicken's back, and then he too becomes fodder for the slaughter,
other chicken's stabbing through his feathers in their effort to claim any pink morsel.
A print of blood forms like a foot. Again and again they strike, like a frenzy of sharks

ripping and tearing at the bleeding body of a swimmer, and yet the injured chicken
refuses to give up his spot in the den, keeps pecking and gulping, shivering with pain
at every stab from his brothers. He leaks blood like the sun. He fills the groove
with his unwritten parable. His cousin watches with eyes like totems. Jenkins

throws down his shovel, makes for the door. He thinks about murder. He thinks
about vegetables and things that will not bleed. He walks back to the childhood
house of his father. The porch sleeps carelessly through his terrible return, a sentry
too long bored by his coming and going. He tracks bright red throughout the house.

9. The Out-House

One strand of concertina-wire
between coast-is-clear and dead.
Thursdays we stir the kettle black latrine
full to the brim like a witch's cauldron
with feces. Some of us try to shit less.
I remember when this was much less complicated.

10. Farming Sagebrush: How to Cash In

God gave him two hands.
He put his hands to the earth.
Nothing happened.

11. The Porch and Where Our Hero Would Kiss the Girl

The smell is must and smoke.
    The smell is clean dusty green. The air
                    is tired
    of too many images, of too sharp metal
    of the oil fires boiling,
    of the wet soil. The rotten boards
               are tired
like porch steps. The fires flick
flaming pebbles of light like retreating visions.
    We smell like huddling rodents.
Jenkins says we are as good as dead.
    Jenkins says we are like impertinent,
              viscous,
              bending,
              flame.
He makes no sense—we believe we are heroes. Jenkins dies right then, a splash of bone and
brain. We live. This is confirmed:
the ridge above the combat is like a porch step,
    I watch men fall,
              I watch Jesus sinking up to his genitals,
the red sea closing, Mohammed punching a tourist,
           then robbing them blind,
              stupid.
            Siddhartha says, sage smoke is a dying mountain, but we
are not listening anymore. We think we hear Mohammed
asking us to leave him to his own punishment.
              We assume it is famine.
It is an eternity until sunrise, and only the smoke and fires
hold off the carnal grip
of the desert. We sleep next to the bodies,
           dig holes next to them to keep warm in the night,
             we are like rodents burrowing into the sand.
         Finally, near the end, I hear the laughter
punching up from the differing shades of rusty blood,
         from the boards themselves.
         Finally the two worlds will touch and separate, and
they sound like the terrible red blood mockery
of every god I have dared pray to.

The Focus of the Thousand Mile Stare

Here's where I say, "Are you scared, man?" I say it the same way every time, and in one minute we will be pushing to the door of the aircraft, our weapon bags partially unzipped, with a magazine slapped tightly and carefully into the chamber. Before we stand, I will look down the line of soldiers and I will think how awful it all is. I will think how unfair it is that we should be the ones, my friends and I, droning over Latin American forests in full combat gear, over wondrous places we will most likely never visit again. Ready to die on foreign, fabulous, soil. We have already written letters home, exchanged them, so that if someone makes it, our final words will exist at least, as apologies. I look over at Mark, his body bathed in the blood red light of the interior lights, his face shaded red and black like a skull, and I shift forward, meaning to ask him if he would personally talk to my parents if I didn't make it back. Instead, I hear those same words come from my mouth and, as always, I feel like it is too soon—I just need one more moment, maybe I can tell Mark not to stand up, tell him that if he stands he will surely die, but there is no time left. We stand and hook our yellow nylon static lines to the long cable running down the aircraft, and we turn toward the rear of the aircraft, toward the opening door. The sound envelopes us, in the real sense of envelopment—it is tangible, it is awful, it is terrifying, and against any sanity, our feet yearn for the space, for the emptiness that is flying and falling both. As always, I count to three, and the first anti-aircraft rounds hit our C-141, and despite my urge to move, a piece of flack buries itself in my cheek the exact same way it always has, and I count to five and we are hit again, and we are moving forward like giggling men, holding on to each other's shoulders as if in mirth, shuffling one, two, one, two, one, two, toward the door, and we are hit again, hard, and I can see gaping holes in the aluminum shell of the aircraft, and I hear the man behind me take a round. I do not turn around. I know who he is; the one I would not talk to on the flight over because he was a pogue officer who had supplanted our squad's SAW rifleman, Antarrios Winters. Just an officer who wanted a medal, who pursued glory and advancement over sanity—a man who died in the blind pursuit of a fucking Combat Infantryman Badge. I knew he would be a danger to my squad, and I resented him, and I resented him his CIB. I hear him gurgle through his awful injuries, and I am wet on the back of my pants, and I know it is blood, and it makes me glad that Winters was not there because I liked him, and I know that I will not look back for anything. It is so fast. Everything is so fast, and so dull. I stumble once, and put my hand out to steady myself, and then I am close, only a few steps from the door. This is it. I count one, two, and Mark is hit, OH GOD, Mark is hit, he is turning for help, his body stumbling backwards clumsily, grabbing for anything, and I move up to hold him, unconsciously thinking that I had given him one of my letters, and I see that his Kevlar vest is empty. He is dead already, but doesn't know it yet, then one, two, he does and his face contorts like I don't know what, and he is falling, and I hold him, but he slips out of my arms, and I grab again, and he is light, oh he is light, empty, and his stuff is on the wall and on the jumpmaster, he is spread like peanut butter over it all, he is just a flack jacket with nothing left to protect, and then I know he is dead, and he does too, finally. I lay him on the floor, but he is blocking the doorway, and I am slipping in the dark—the green light for go is blinking and it goes red, red, red, and we push and kick him, we push him out the door, poor dead Mark, out the door, and I follow, maybe anxious to find redemption, or death, or both.

This is how it always happens, how I have become accustomed to that night, but this time I count one, two, and no bullets bang on the walls, and the officer behind me just bumps into me, whispers "Sorry." We are moving slowly, I can hear my breath in my chest, can feel the air moving like water past my lips. For this one time Mark exits, and things are moving again, and there is no time to count the rounds beating against the shell of the plane because someone is tapping on my back hard, and I am off balance, and cold like I have never been before, and the world is spinning, and I look back for someone to help me breathe again. I know what this is all about. I know not to look down, but I can feel my throat constricting, and the veins bulging in panic in my neck, and I know that there will be no me down there, just an empty, whistling vest filled with the darkest, darkest blood ever, and none of it going where it is supposed to go, and I hope sometimes that this were the truth, and all the others just bad dreams. I am on my back, and I can feel how my vest is sinking down in the chest because there is nothing there to hold it up, and I don't want to die here, my last view of this world boots clumping past, stained with my blood. This is all there ever is. Somebody please, let me out into that rush of air, into that pretty abyss.

II. Those Stains Will Never Come Out

Golem

This Golem awakes from soil and cobbled stone
in Stare Mesto, Prague. His long fugue sleep, a mystery,
a brown and dusty apprenticeship to woe and famine

and indenture. I'm just telling you, like Jan Hus the zealot,
I am standing erect and awake in Staromestke Namesti, and
like Golem, I feel great sorrow for wasted and burning years,

each folded into molten obscurity. You have to watch the clock tower
in the square closely—is time's arrow spinning feathers first, pointing
the razor end at our dark history? This Golem, rising like smoke from

the crypt of my walking sleep, mouthless, asks the
pointed question: "Where the fuck are the women?"
Let me tell you, he is asking something else of us

buddyo. He is asking what we are doing out here in the hollow
crowds of distorted souls. This city makes me never want to sleep
again. Pay attention to this history—the old Moldau river will eat your

illusions up, little SallyMaryNancy. Believe me, this city sleeps and sleeps
and sleeps with one eye open: it watches—eastern bloc paranoia burning
from dark windows and silent streets. In the end, you have to dig

deep to find them, those bohemian voices—open any door and
walk into an ancient world of smoke and dark and noise. They will
be there, looking you in the eye, deciding who you are.

How to Look West From Mount Pleasant, Utah

Your brushstrokes licked dryly at cheap canvas
in raspy, natural swipes; on brown and green Army
shirts stretched between boards--some obscure affront
to the precipitous mountains of the Wasatch Front.

The weeping of your brush was nearly audible, one
treacherous vision of the world after another. Your
first painting was cartoonishly symmetrical. A row
of hills like the inverted udders of the sows you raised.

These unfinished paintings left unfinished. A legacy
of unharvested fruit, an Indian Summer snowstorm,
a B-2 flying in low, bringing with it a modern nuclear
dogma. A field lingers, white with alkaline salt, where

the bones of a dinosaur wait, feet up and eyes rolling
in the back of their sockets. What remains is a farmhouse,
or church, rising from a bitter hillside; it is buried in sharp
snowdrifts. There are plows and shredders and combines

buried there. Their metallic ears point to the empty sky
like cactus. You are there, on the steps looking off, away
from the mountains west, at what remains of the frontier;
or maybe, at the last frozen crow, climbing up from

the dead barley and hay. There are no sounds there.
No radio ever whispered to the three sets of children
growing all wildly different. Who was there to remind
you of the year? Was it 1943 or 1945? These numbers

must have seemed arbitrary--a gift from the future.
Maybe you are not looking, but listening, to the sound
of one million four-hundred thousand lost voices.
The questions remain the same. How will this be written

to sound important, like the grey caribou is important,
or the trap-door spider? Important like cheese, in soft
curds, stirring in stainless steel, tripping over and burping
their way among milk solids. I would ask why you chose

the color purple for your mountains, why make
sky the color of granite, rivers the tan yellow shade of a bruise
of a bruise, amber for a bank of clouds. It could have been
anyone's bruise color, but it felt like mine. How could

you keep your back turned to that color, and the reaching,
the way the mountains reached for your shoulder, to touch
you, saying *hey animal, that is my abdomen you stand on,*
or *This bald patch* (you know, the one to the west

of the Snake River) *itches like a mother-fucker.* Even
on the porch, your hands are curled to the reins of a horse,
or to the huge ladle in the cheese factory, or around the neck
of a chicken. The house behind you seems empty. Painted

empty in moribund fascination, painted empty among squadrons
of children, empty and hollow like a casket, and yes, there is a better
metaphor but I have seen that house you grew up in and it seemed
drafty and wet and empty, like a casket, the wooden kind

that lets one's remains leak out after only one week. That
is why you stand out in the cold November looking
west, away from the mountains, toward what remains
of the frontier, away from the house you were raised in,

and where you raised children, and where on some evenings
your wife would wash your aching feet--peeling off the moldy
boots, whispering *Poor, poor Daddy* from the milking stool.
You stayed home, the only male left to listen to a silence

so profound it maddened the hounds, and the moose,
and pulled trees down in squealing ecstasy. The white
of the snow seems dirty around the porch steps, as if the world
was set upon something else. A river ran nearby, the sound

of it melting was morose and languid. Are you listening
to it complain? Your expression is one I have seen before—
it is the blank expression that pursed your lips and wrinkled
your brow whenever you tried to solve the triangle peg

puzzle that Grandma gave you. You laughed when I told
you a peg was missing, when I said it was impossible.
You said, *That remains to be seen.* Now, when I look
at this painting, I wonder what would have happened
if instead of looking west, you had been looking
down, at what the color of soil looked like on canvas.

China Girl

You will not have heard of her,
her greatness not born of American
roots, she is what we sailed
on razor seas to create: a fearless

lover and gymnast and spirit,
a tireless woman born of splits
and flips and twists and innumerable
broken bones and torn ligaments and

strained tendons, a girl who knows
what she wants and is not afraid
to smile fiercely when she gets it,
a girl who laughs at small mistakes,

embraces competitors in genuine
comradeship, a girl who will nail
you to the balance beam if given
a chance. She is a patriot, a national hero.

The east is rising under a new sun,
her people swelling and morphing behind
the constraints of borders. The Koreans
and Romanians remain grim, their ties

to cold war fancies still fresh.
Watch the tapes of Atlanta and Sydney
and you will see the change in China
Girl: she is an oleander blossom, she is

an Olympian who will smile bright
from the podium the smile of what
we have always thought was only
American; a smile of dominance, surety,

arrogance even, and if you look around
at those watching with you,
you will see that cold China
is no more, that cold China

is rising to steal from us our freedom
to pursue happiness without
ever firing a single shot, without
ever brandishing her titanium sword.

Alpen Suiss Jungfrau

God was invented here,
as were avalanche breaks
and the wristwatch. Time,
inevitability, then time again.

The dogmatic tourists are
gone now—only the hardened
granite nailed golems of
the Alps remain, der Berner

Oberland, slow moving and
glacial and frigid. I could stay
here, in the turning leaves—you
know, the generic beauty of green

and gold and red, with cattle
chewing cud on the sloped side
of a mountain. Their hooves
dig in, they are like obese

and stinking spiders hanging
by tongues from sweeps
of yellow hay. The farmers still
scythe for them in sweeping dances.

I could stay and watch, maybe join in,
but my godforsaken heart can't take it.

First

The well dressed Hispanic
man has his hot coffee
and is heading back to work.

He switches his coffee to his
weak hand and reaches
for the knob to leave as two

men in ties approach. They
have nothing in their
hands, yet the man makes a

gallant effort to open the door
wide for them, his coffee
spilling hot on his hand as he

fumbles with the door and the
newspaper pinched under
his arm. The men power through

the entryway, speaking loudly,
and head straight to the
counter. It is such a small thing,

this courtesy.

Dublin

I don't mind how you paint my soul,
As long as you get my tie correct. —James Joyce

This wet journey-town, woolen
and soggy like sheep farts,

long in tooth and silence for
the wake of numb Finnegan, how

like Joyce to take the joy out
of a joyless place. From this

window I can see pictures of you
in every raindrop. And I know

how many rooms you have in
your flat by counting those

sooty and cold chimney pots.
And yes, if you have been paying

attention: if you have not nodded
off in Leon's favorite chair (oh, that

is so like you to always think of it as
your favorite chair!) is it really

necessary to tell you that outside
it is raining down buckets of sky?

I am as close to you now as I will
ever be, standing where you stood,

but I still have nagging questions
to ask, like, where are those poor

hookers, and where are the good bars.
Tell me Jim, was it by accident or by

design that the water of your city
tastes faintly of sulphur?

Sunshine Running Wild

Beyond his parentage, Sunshine
has a heavy handful of used tissue paper
and he is going to put it into his mouth.

I am close enough to stop him, but I
am curious and bored, and too late anyway,
because hey the deed is done, and he is already

looking for bugs and cigarette butts
under the splintery park benches. He is
rank with turds and his arm looks like

he has crammed it into a gallon of chocolate
ice cream. Too far away, Mom and Dad Hippy
are carelessly smoking dope, their cream pit bull

leashed and sleeping beneath them.
I watch Sunshine devour more horrible
things, hear him fill his britches again,

but when he makes a break for the busy street,
I finally put my copy of *Catch-22* down and spill
my tepid coffee in my rush to save the day.

She Dances on Vulcanized Rubber

And her people came, the new heroes of Honky-Tonk, the knights of the New Deal, the inertial generation at work on the American dream. She was born with the Nuclear Age rehearsed to her in dreams amid woolen sheets and iron heavy water. Her morning newspapers were parables of the Titanic and Mussolini, her husband one of the rare survivors of both Great Wars. Pearl danced to the music of Louis Armstrong with men lucky enough to have limbs. She danced in black high heels during the Great Depression, she danced the Rag-Tag with her man on the hardwood dance floors littered with streamers and balloons and pools of liquor back when Patton was king. Her picture is black and white in a time when the blue of the sky, the green of the trees, the red of raw hands, and the brown of the earth were a birthright. She reminds us that the gray world of Life magazine was the most colorful age of all. She could buy a bag of candy for an egg stolen from the nest. For her misery was a patient constancy. George Orwell's 1984 was horror, not familiarity. She recites the death of her brother, tells of his closed coffin draped in a flag. Just whose body was in there anyway? She believes he is out there somewhere, like the spear-bearing Roman soldier, cursed to roam the earth until the apocalypse. Her generation birthed the curse words of creationism, her peers drew straws for combat or genius.

And in her last confusion, people came rushing around her, long practiced in the habit of abomination, the capturers of the Mastodon, the creators of the lock and the key, the builders of the Empire State, and she worked the dance-floor oblivious. The fruits of convenience, the aged and youthful, the road work for the Roaring Twenties, one near-century-long-groomed-cruise, neatly joined like her two rows of false interlocking teeth. Pearl built the tree house with her own hands, and was there to see the hideout of her children fall. She is free of your silly conscience, she is worthy of a soldier's praise. She is dancing on a heel of vulcanized rubber, she is the ballet's instrument bidding this strange world
nighty-night.

--for Pearl Peterson

How Plastic Feels About The Sun

My back will ache with the weight of a thousand dead men,
life will roll like a tomato can, down an aisle, filled
with old women tending to pale-faced, awful children
who wonder at the hatred the sun holds for tin foil.

Island storms will roll away the soil from the roots of tomato plants
exposing blank shards of betrayal, how empty the world is,
no wonder the sun burns hatred on every tin roof, on every back,
on every eaten prune; how crude we see the tools of evolution

lying with our blank world, so opposed to the empty eyes of sharks.
Our candy will not digest, it will rot like holiday gravy, in zip-lock bags
uneaten, neglected. The prunes will revolt with crude tools and forks
beating down the doors of ancient cupboards, killing beans and soda cans,

their sweetness pooling like gravy, mopped up with Christmas stockings.
How like the earth to ignore this, to leave us to our nuclear tantrums,
to make us gods for inventing aluminum, to build the doors to our own coffins.
What good beasts of burden we make, what great backs to break. Turn

ignorant children squalling at the sight of science, turn god against creation,
like the backs of a thousand dead men aching for some yoke against domesticity;
anything to fill the empty cavity of the world with all the materials of the awful end.
We refuse to tend to stupid children, who are wiping tears on the aprons of old women.

Those stains will never come out.

III. Mormon Boy

Mormon Boy

Mormon Boy follows the flat print of moon boots in the snow, a collie slobbering and grinning by his side. He steps uncertainly, his arms wind-milling occasionally, the fat pack of his ink stained harness shifting on his thighs with cool sighs of newspaper and rubber bands and bright orange plastic bags. He throws his papers like he skips rocks—quick and tightly spinning to thump loudly on screen doors.

The sun is combing its hair, looking in the mirror, rubbing its fingers over hot teeth, spitting phlegm in the sink of the galaxy. The sun stares into the sink, eyes as red and bloody and hung-over as time, slow to appear for the Mormon Boy and his dog. The sky is up and cheerful already, white and blue and cold—a reverse impression that mirrors the snowy fleets of white as far as the boy can see. His nose is running with the cold and his numb fingers have trouble clutching the sides of the paper harness, but he is unstoppable. He will deliver them all. He is the best paper boy in town—the papers always get delivered and even the huge bang of his throws are tolerated by the sleepy housewives and the humorless farmers with their black coffee.

Sometimes the Mormon Boy cries miserably to himself if the snow is deep and heavy—his legs are short and the snow is high, and sometimes he even gets frustrated enough to kick his beloved black collie in the ribs when he cries, one leg after another raised high and dropped, raised high and dropped, his tears angry white lines on the red of his cheeks. He is dumbfounded by a world that allows a good boy to suffer this hardship. Mormon Boy believes he doesn't deserves this. His sorrow is huge and wounded and he laments his own terrible plight with the power of time's children. No one deserves to wade through snow for eighty bucks a month, and him only six years old! and cold! and forced to kick his beloved dog in the ribs! And Mormon Boy will never know that the seven years he walks this route will be the longest tenure with one company he will ever have.

But he is saving! Saving! Saving! when he is not stealing candy from Olson's Market, and when he is not buying Swedish gummy fish for Robyn (she kisses him!) and Tara (the cutest girl in school!). And he is tithing too, making sure of his place in the baptismal font, where at eight he will be dipped by his solemn father. When the time comes, Mormon boy will wonder: why did he kick the dog, and why did he let Jeffrey touch his dinger, and why does he spit in his baby sister's milk, and is it bad that he eats his boogers, and does little baby Jesus know he picks and eats every one? On baptism day, he will see the asbestos ceiling tilt, and as the cold water envelopes him, he will wonder if maybe little mister perfect, Kevin Taylor, whom he hates with all his little Mormon Boy might, was right, if maybe the baptismal font is where they drown the little boys who just aren't cutting it.

Where to Find Work in Natrona, Wyoming

Natrona remains a mystery,
a Highway 287 remnant
of a time when Wyoming
satisfied herself, with solitude.
Population five. This

should say it all. You
walk through railway
cinders to a grocery
store disguised as a gas stop.
You wear the same shoes

you always have—or maybe,
boots that chafe your ankle
with twenty-seven years of
sweat accumulated under this
same sign. Natrona mocks you,

with a population exactly
one thousandth its elevation.
Here, dust floats like a fog
over everything, but ultimately
obscures only the fact that there

is nothing to see but horizon. This
is a family thing—you run the
store because you always have.
In Natrona, generations
are measured in a dry, leathery

handshake. You bide time
with a home veterinary guide
and come off sure you could
operate on the broken foreleg
of a horse with no problems.

Later as the sun sets, you turn on the
radio that is next to the Ring-Dings,
near the window that looks out on
the highway, and hum along
to a song you know the words to.

Being There

This alienation is for you.
Let the grass-cutter sharpen
his shears on the metal grates
of sewage drains, let him fish
for pennies with pink globs
of Bazooka Joe chewing gum,

let Peter Sellers fall down
the stairs like a crippled clown, let
him watch Eve hike up her
dandy skirts with hands hooked
by Autism and stiff drinks.
I like to watch, Eve, your Mantra.

One side of town versus
the other, a gardener hiding,
another gardener tending to the cemetery.
The bricklayer drinks Power-Ade,
the blacksmith no longer exists
so we won't mention him,
the carpenter nails his hand to the wall
and does the Hootchie-Kootchie with
a hot babe, or is it the Fandango?
The man on the watchtower is
looking the wrong way,
a police officer is watching him
missing it all, bellicose and seething;
the flight recorder is fitted
with a cultural empathy device,
Superman has joined Tarzan in
the jungle, and on the other side of town
the electrician is wiring your home
with an holographic fireplace.

The gardener mows the grass
over his ancestors, he trims
along the headstones, and
during breaks, he sets his cigar
on the hood of his mower, where
it vibrates and sparks in the
heat of a crippling summer.

They will tell you to
keep the butcher away
from the chicken and the pork,
take the rubber gloves from
the garbage-man and give them
to the proctologist, resort
to savagery, write a trite and cliché poem
that has the moon and a rose in it—
let the grass-cutter walk his rounds,
let him lay on his work, let him
cut every single stalk of grass
the same length, and let him look
you straight in the eye when he says,
"I wanted to be a gardener,
not a grass-cutter."

They will tell you
that this isn't a poem
at all, that it is
an allegory, a penis joke,
a list of names
and occupations.
I will lie and tell you I thought
it up on my lunch hour,
over a turkey and cheese
Lunchable.
Someone, please!
Take this pen away
before I damage my
reputation.

Two Cats, an Hundred Roaches, a Dog

We bumped the rental truck into the carport on the first night,
let the fetid wet of the late summer wash our stink from the vehicles—
a great gas soup of body odor and cigarettes and wet dog swirling
into the night. The electricity was off, and there were dead roaches strewn

everywhere—we both agreed it was a bad sign, though neither of us
spoke of it. I hadn't slept in forty-two hours, but it was up to me
to find the fuse box with the weak yellow light of a dying flashlight.
In the darkened shed, I was frightened near to pissing myself by an opossum

that hissed at me and ran off into the Florida night. I opened the fuse
box just as the flashlight died, and only by feel did I know the great
disturbance to a roach family I was the cause of—when I entered
the newly dim kitchen, I could see clearly enough to knock two

of the ugly creatures from my leg hairs, and clean their three squashed
relatives from the soles and padding of my sandals. You were taking
the Red Bulls and vodka from the car and putting them in the mustard yellow
refrigerator, carefully bringing the cats in, putting a bed out for the dog.

You were always vigilant with the care of your animals, and the light
from the fridge showed me the life we had agreed upon: the long future
of allergies for me, the passive aggressive silences from you, and it was
then that I began to really hate you for failing to love me like I deserved.

I swept the house free of the dead insects while you calmed your animals,
then I began to unload the truck alone in the dark rain—determined to have
a bed for us at least, somewhere for you and I to let the magnitude of our situation
press down upon us. We were doomed already, a thousand miles from home,

and I look back now to those first nights, how the rain began to fall softly
on the tin roof, how it broke into a thunderous downpour with hard lightning,
and I think that I should have let that shack burn to the ground when you closed
the fridge door and the blue shout of electricity began to sizzle and snap

along a short in the wires—and as the fire began to crawl up the peeling flowers
of the wallpaper, your silhouette began to dance uselessly in the new light.

Making Out in Cars with Bucket Seats and Other Tales of Woe

As always, the flashing blue and reds catch me off guard,
as if I were new to this teenage fumble and clutch, and our
zippers and buckles betray our shaking hands, our blue jeans

grow thick and oily, loath to swallow our legs again, her crimson
lipstick a clown's smudge touchup to my face. At the last our jeans
are force-fed enough to cover her hoo-ha and my shamed boner,

but late, too late, we are doomed! Her bra straps hang like wings
from her tight t-shirt armholes, and fly she would, letting my bones
be worried and gnawed by the indigo hulk of the officer approaching,

authority growing by the step, and isn't this the limit! Same cop as last
night, but different girl! I walk the line as my new ex studies the slow approach
of disappointed cars that circle and leave. I follow the light as her auburn

hair is framed by the glow of a cigarette, unsanctioned, in my Prelude,
and then I am deemed sober, but indigo hulk senses an attitude and burns
me with twenty awkward questions about last night, loud enough to squeeze

dead my last chance with Red, my secret out, her escape a certainty,
but that isn't enough for the incredible blue dick of a cop--I am squeezed
for sure as the search of my backpack commences with a tattered copy

of the "Anarchist's Cookbook," then degrades to an array of loose condoms
and bits of weed and seeds lining the bottom. The text is indeed the copy
stolen from the library, so there's small trouble there, then there's the dope,

but hey, I've seen crimson hot five-oh heat before, and no cop paperwork
would convict on those tiny bits of party favors, and Red, being no dope,
opens my car door and starts sprinting away into the night, her silhouette

flashing purple and black in the swirl of ruby and sapphire lights, long hair
swinging like a middle finger, and then I am running too, my dark silhouette
a bull's-eye, a giant target, a free pass for a cop busting his first-kill cherry,

and will the absurdity never stop! I run right down the middle of the dirt road
to a rusting bridge, until the bustling lights of the law enclose me in the cherry
bosom of their authority. And it is not lost on me either that if I had simply

bought American, those bucket seats of the Honda would've been the wide
bench seats of a Nova, with room to make love like adults--supine and simple,
hidden away from the red sweep of lights, out to make us tremble and shrink.

Old Girlfriends Never Die

When I met you, you were a confused schoolgirl—eating poorly, kind of dirty. You were a deception in hand-painted clogs, holding your knees in a queer raped fragility, watching me carve redwood totems, turning deep side-cuts into fairies, at your whim. You hadn't quite gotten the personal hygiene trick turned yet, and you smelled sour like sweaty, end- of-the-ski-season down coats. You said, *I'm not going to fuck you tonight*, on our first date, waving the smoke from a bummed cigarette away from your oddly shaped face, and I knew that I could have you then if I wanted. Then you kissed me, and awkwardly held my hand like an escaped convict hand-cuffed to a dead body. I couldn't help but notice that you had the veiny and shaking hands of a heroin addict at twenty-one. And a big scar on your shoulder that you never tried to hide. You wore halter-tops and sleeveless dresses, defects evident with the same brashness that a politician proudly showing his war wounds would have.

But god you were cute, and mysterious, and mean to me. It never occurred to me that you only loved rock stars. After nights of manhattans I would wake early and make you breakfast, the dusty smell of my apartment mingling with pork drippings—the house cold with the putridly wet air of San Francisco. And you never even said thank you. I showed you my favorite spot, above the surf that pounded in relentlessly against the scarred and pitted sea wall. The sea had a grip there I told you, a grip that would ultimately pull the earth down with it, drowning the world. I wonder, toward the end, when you knew I knew of the other guy, did you ever think that I would push you off? You sat way behind me on the wet fingers of the sand cactuses, and I put my feet over the edge, and thought about jumping, and I don't know if you knew this, but I had an opportunity before we had even kissed to steal your underpants, and I took it.

Wilco

I hear the gnashing of your *summer*
teeth with every note—you are the sweet
accompaniment to my last duplicitous

relationship, my long list of conquests,
you make me ache like the chainsaw spurting
oil as it rips into the fragrant bark of an ancient

sequoia. A man like me, you would say,
shouldn't be so sensitive to his own
sins—you might even recommend that

next time I stick my dick into my long term
girlfriend instead of haggard and diseased women
at the bar. And you are right, as always, but I can't

help feeling the sharp and bright ache of conquest
potential sitting at the stool next to me, and I can't
help being the coward who turns his women into

cuckolds simply because I am too pusillanimous
(a word the last one defined for me as I studied for the GRE)
to split, to run, before I use my treachery as a tool

for them to leave me, to give me the awful power
of the abandoned. I am unburdened, and yes,
I resent women who are smarter than me,

and I bang women much dumber than me, and
yes, you should sing a song about men like me
who ruin women, but you won't descend

to my level of play, and you won't quit lecturing me
with sound until I reach over and let *The Flaming Lips*
quiver and smack and shake me like I really deserve.

Where We Are Going With This

—after Jim Simmerman

These things are what I am: a mouse in a field, eaten
by a coiling snake. I am the sound of last muffled shrieks
until the rodent is yanked from the white mouth and fangs.
I am the mouse with venom wrestling in his veins.

I am my father and mother, I am a grimacing farmer
watching children wrestle with natural selection, a mouse
and snake—nature's oldest cliché. I am Ronald Reagan,
forgetful, a lover of jelly beans, missiles, and old mother

Nancy. I am Nancy Alper, my first kiss, and great winding
highways. I am the man who says *Wo ist der bahnhoff*
when I am looking for the toilet. I am a man who knows
this is incorrect. I am a poet who compares Nancy Reagan

and rattlesnakes. I am a poet who compares himself
to his parentage—the oldest road in a Wyoming town,
a gravel street dusted with old cowboy sweat, oily
cattle blood, road apples, the whole Shoshone nation,

and my bloodline. And I am other things. I am five years old
and I am in love for the second time, I am waiting by the swings
for that kiss. I am how that kiss tickled and that tongue bucked.
I am a dry map of the sweating asphalt, the bleachers, the secrecy,

and the shiny new tiny hard-on. And the search for the same Zing!
Pow! Bang! of that kiss; a lifetime of pursuit. Questions like:
am I the boy with the slingshot? Am I Mr. Fielding, bad breath
and lollipops and the licorice smell of yearning? The surfer,

kowabunga dude, riding over the fin of a shark--what carapaced
menace has depraved Fortuna spun my way? I am Chuck Taylor
basketball shoes, I am a curmudgeon, a bright slice of orange,
a sewer rat, a hat knocked off in the wind, a lonely cowboy,

out of place in a gray city. I am saffron mixed with salt—Moby
finger-painting in a blue swimming pool, curved into the shape
of a hard chlorine dinosaur. Do you see the makeup, the avarice,
the just-getting-by of who I am—do you hope this is all going somewhere?

The Karma Suite

To live in the fog of San Francisco is to write
a poem about San Francisco—to add to the palimpsest
of the past couple of decades your own footnote, to add your
own layer to the last medley of bad poetry, to become trite

and melancholy along with grad students trying to be Ferlinghetti
or Ginsberg or Snyder. Failing that, you may join the illiterate
and mirror Neal Cassidy *On the Road,* or Neal Cassidy
Electric Kool-Aid Acid Test. You may eat spaghetti

in smarmy bistros in the North Beach, tear
croissants to shreds in cafes next to City Lights
Bookstore, drop sunshine acid in the park
and roll the hippies near the Haight. You will fear

authority, seek out your own kind on the trains
from the Sunset district and Cole Valley. You will
become the last remnants of a lost society. You will
seek out some safety in numbers, the coffee stains

of your self-importance a prayer to the deaf ears
of the lost generation. You will step over the relics
of this great city with every step you take on the way
to get a beer or a smoke. Soon, you realize the queers

are the only real artists left in the city, and in spite of this,
you will write your desperately cliché poem in a café
as cliché as you find yourself to be, you will look for material
on the walls of every men's room you find, the balled fist

in your corduroy pocket just a refusal to give up, to go away.
You will write poems that are vivid copies of the Beats, maybe
better versions of *Howl* and *Khaddish.* You will call it practice,
but in your heart you know it is plagiarism—a bitter bay

area form of art addiction, or creative infection. Your last poem
will steal a desperate cry for love from an American Indian student,
his loud poetry written in cursive on the bathroom wall at SF State.
Defeated, you will watch your city disappear in the mirror, and ten
days later, in a dirty spoon diner just outside a truck-stop in Flagstaff,
your pen will finally pour its ink into a poem that came from within.

IV. The Best Man In All The World

The Best Man in All the World

This is not some carnival dream, some abysmal side-show, some rotten
place for the forlorn and envious; it is not some sad story to be pulled
out like a deck of cards at a martyr's tea party, or a fifth grade excuse
to use the potty, to carve bad words on the stall door, to get caught.

It is a Taiwanese elephant ride, a 50 cent matinee, where the broken
springs in the seats whisper for sex, and a bone thin man with popcorn
and soda begs to sodomize. The best man in all the world knew what
a ride it could be. Never a moment of self-doubt, like a stupid puppy,

oblivious to the point of being dangerous, lovable. A twenty-three year
mule ride, unpredictable, exhilarating, uncomfortable, and silly. The best
man in all the world sat in the stirrups of an Arabian pure-bred like a lost king
and pretended it was the sagging back of a Quixotic mule, just for a laugh.

This is not a boat on the sea slowly gaining water, not a child-proof medicine
bottle, or a smelt factory running on soft coal. It is never weak coffee, never
$2.13 an hour jobs, nor is it the darkness of the cold desert, or the sound of tracer
rounds smoking and popping in the chest of dead young men. And it is not

the absence of beauty, the loss of a friend, nor the empty cavity of a forgotten
tooth. No, it is just simple loss. It is the indentions in an old carpet where
the missing love-seat once sat, where you and countless others lost their virginity.
It is getting stoned with the best man and having only six dollars of his brother's

money to buy tacos. It is not being able to order, giving the clerk the six
dollars and walking out, to return with no tacos no money no idea of where
you have been. It is hiding beer in a creek at the side of a road, returning later
to see some Wyoming farmer walking away with it. It is never waiting for a ride

while hitch-hiking, whiskey sours for breakfast, lunch, it is bed and breakfasts,
cheating on room rates, it is a brutal basketball game next to a gay beach in New
Hampshire. And it is also hiding from the house mother among the liquor bottles
in a closet, while she talks of redemption, private-school manners, noise, and gastric

problems. It is waking up to a piano piece the best man in all the world composed
purely by memory, Bass ale, beach boiled lobsters, that piano piece lost forever,
a porch swing inside a house on the beach. It is writing a poem with the best man
in the world, then leaving him forever to board a bus, a train, then a bus again

for the Army and war. It is never seeing him standing again, never jumping
off bridges into icy water, never drinking vodka and tea, never listening to the Beatles.
He loses in the end, if that's what you are wondering. No Spanish soap opera here.

The best man shrivels up in front of me, he dissipates, he fills the room with only his
misunderstood presence. The best man flips me off at odd times just to let me know

he is still hidden there. It is him doing these things from a paralytic coma for four years
just to let me know things are A-OK in bestmansville. Then, towards the end,
it is a lunch of Chateaubriand cooked rare with the best man in all the world
in a wheelchair. It is matching the stares stare for stare, it is wanting to pick him

up, carry him anywhere, keep carrying him, never stop. It is trading in those sexy
springs in the chairs at the matinee for those in foul-odored trucks and buses. Asking
for Portland, Maine, or Boston and getting rehab rooms in Denver or San Diego.
It is believing that thirty mile an hour car accidents do not stop the best man in all

the world, forget the plate in his head, forget the broken eyes, forget the catheter,
the hospitals the doctors the doubt the white rooms the face that is not the best man
in all the world's but is. The best man in all the world starts at the end and ends
with the beginning. He waits for Boulder, stamps his own expiration date before

finishing dinner, never even offers the liquid food being pumped through a tube
into his belly a drop of gastric juice. The best man in all the world acknowledges
the Arabian, finds nothing funny about the mule. The best man in all the world
is the way anti-aircraft rounds empty the Kevlar vest of a friend, it is how it feels

to slip in the blood, the way you follow the dead boy out the door, it is tracer rounds
cutting holes in your parachute, it is falling into battle, landing in a field in darkness
only lit by explosions, it is only being able to think about the best man in all the world,
hoping it will be your last thought, the only thought. It is never forgetting the last time

you saw him standing, at the bus station in Colorado Springs, it is the look
on his face, it is not being sure of what that sad expression should tell you.

The Opening and Closing Thighs of the Universe

We will speak loudly tonight, under a tent of smoke
and booze and music. Like under-arm deodorant scraped with
razors or just one long worn out strip of Andrew Wyeth
cartoons the way he wanted,; no humor, no joke.

We will fall into each other, hoping to get off right
the way the movie stars do, me Archie Bunker, you
the Calgon Lady, our sex made into quibbling over just whose
nightmare we were living, and who gets off who tonight.

You are watching me die by being with me—watching
me shed a million cells for every second of my life.
Just like the way we looked for the dead arcing to the earth
among the debris and smoke and flames, searching
for bodies plummeting through the television sights.
Into our living room, the space shuttle is falling.

Curtain Calls

She will transform
right before your eyes;
from dog to soldier to Portia
to ER nurse, to forlorn

lover. She is the leaves
on the burning bush—colors
like all the light from the
spectrum, falling in sweeps

and circles, then rising up
again, touching stem to branch,
reborn—a pulsing kaleidoscope
of mutability. She is stern,

she is serene, she is joyous
in turn, this great play shaping
her moods, the stage a
partnership between immortal arts.

In her Sylvia, all the canine world
runs under the imagined legs
of a dachshund, the rusty
Scumperdog of Silverlake licking

and piddling his way through
the same acts of this play. You
will try to tell the difference, find
human in dog, dog in human, but

you will fail. They are tied into
one another, the playful dog the great
progeny of the wise evolutionary play
of Dauphin. Ultimately, we learn to watch

the slow turning of the leaves as an art as well—
just as the transition from theater to tree
to canine is another part of the progression.
Watch her from afar, the energy of the sky

sparking and snapping with her transient
soul—she will allow the curtain to fall
around her, but the light of her illusory talent
will shine from under the velvet slits in cloth.

The roar of the ovation will frighten you
out of her world, she will become mortal again,
a strange girl on a stage, both she and the circle of light
insecure, madly trying to match each turning color.

And someday, you too will have a
story about the day you met her—at
a party, the store, at lunch. The story about
the day you touched the flame of fame,

and it was cold and sharp to the touch.

Children and Blind-men and Gods

It is the French-Canadians
and the women from Tulsa
and Malaga and sober Sonoma
wine country that turn a mountain
excursion into a love affair. On
the grassy slopes of Gimmewald,
Switzerland, every one of my female
students flirt harmlessly with me,
 but even so, my peripheral vision
is alert and watching for a peek of their
perfect tummies in tiny t-shirts. We
are sliding down the mountainside,
laughing at each wide-eyed,
panicked expression. I slide by,
further than even the bravest

boy. How I envy their young bodies!
They watch with their mouths
open and their tongues clicking
silver studs against their unstained teeth.
And I am watching young
Caron, a slip in my pedagogy,
a failure, a love, an unquenchable
thirst—her body tight and soft
and there for the taking if I could
only ask for it. Her tiny belly peeks
out from under a pink shirt that
reads,

Sometimes I like to ride the cable-cars.
I don't know where they are going.
Sometimes I get lost, but that's OK.

and I love her for the sweet
intelligence of it all. In
the bright sunlight, my guilt
asks me to keep sliding, past
vanilla cattle clinging to the mountain
by their black hooves, beyond
the chocolate cabin, to disappear
off the end of the world, flipping end
over end in one of histories greatest pratfalls.

I am sliding down beyond them all,
the dry hay a syrupy lubricant,
and the students simply smoke pot;
hydroponic *White Giant*, barely noticing,
carefree and hardly aware that I
am watching. Like Mr. Magoo, I realize
that I am not to be trusted. Children and blind
men and gods, one aloof and uninterested,
one clumsy with granite and sky
and pencil shale and quartz lines drawn
slow as time through pressurized volcanic

rock. I wonder how much of this
is by design. Surely the Alps were formed
on purpose, and the glaciers, the great
master carving knife, the terrible
destroyer of giants, a mistake?
The back of my pants are filled
with grass and hay and my legs
are muddied and briny with sweat,
and for the first time in my life,
I feel like becoming a farmer
like my father. Am I being silly
now or is my desire to milk cows
a premonition? These young women!

Tonight, as always, in a tavern appropriately
separated from them, I will order in German—eine
Hefeweisen, bitte! And I will drink Rugenbrau
and Absinthe, and I will look at the mountains like
an ex-lover—I will know every contour
of their face, yet they will seem
fabulously foreign and dangerous.

When Abigail Comes

You can see her struggle with life
even in her calmer moments;
a fire burning in this three
pounds of human flesh, a soul crying

silently a banshee's wail: *I Have Arrived.*
And I Am Early. You can see the mute
sound of her voice clutched hard in her
fists, the immense power of her arrival like

a summoning to gods and angels,
a peal of the highest bell in the
great castle of the universe.
She is the child spirit fumbling

in a bright red and malfunctioning
body, a bit of ignobility for her
to suffer, just a small price to pay for
a shot at mortality, a quick in and

out to see what all the fuss is about.
And god, is she beautiful. It is a sight
to see, this glorious girl-child, pre-
language, pre-cognition, pre-despair,

struggling for the chance to be what
we all take for granted. She has
come early for us, with lessons
burned hard into her DNA—look closely

and you will see that under the waxy
paper of her skin, behind the gray and
black of her eyes; a Giant is rising.
The jerk and slap of her tiny arms

and legs is a physical reckoning—
she will carry this struggle with
existence, this wrestling with angels, like
a sword sheathed for all the rest of her life.

--for Abigail

Reflections

She looks at herself in the hallway mirror
and is pleased with what she sees—the
soft burnt milk of her skin, the new door
to her maidenhood shaved into a perfect

triangle. When she leans back with her hands
on her boyish hips, she sees what eager men
see—the angles perfect for gravity's hands to sand
her adolescence into adult sexuality. Her long dark

hair falls just past her tightening nipples, straight
and true and created solely as a frame for her poorly
concealed sins. Her splayed feet grip hardwood space
with hot pink certainty, her nails mooring her

to place as surely as metal pin to hard oak.
She plumps her breasts with both cupped
hands just as she notices the darkly open
window, and next door, the form of her new

neighbor, the track star. She covers herself with the tangles
of her hair and runs to her room, her hands not enough
to hide her shame. Under her bedclothes, she tingles
with this first touch from the eyes of a man. In the night

outside, a dog barks at the swish of a passing car,
and from the basement, she hears her father's muffled
cough. The cool bedding holds her down, and she wonders,
is this the end, or is this the beginning, of her new life?

Ode to Olivia's Sweet Ass in Soccer Shorts

The men give her room the first
time—she's just a girl on the adult coed
soccer team, harmless and cute in lengthy
blonde corn-rows. The first time

she shakes them, they think it has to be a fluke,
no way, the next time they will be ready.
But look! They are shook again, and off
goes Olivia and her sweet ass, hair

flopping on her liquid shoulders, fast to
the dumbfounded goalie, past the yellow
crossbars, the worn net, and none of
them to stop her before I can stand

and scream GOOOOAAAALLL! like
a crazed Mexican. If she could only
see what I see! Olivia, The Liver,
Lit, Olive, Livey, O, Olie, Litgo, all

of her names, the sum of all the women
she is and will be, captured beneath the fire
red shirt and the peek of floral tattoo
hidden just under the elastic of her white
and perfect soccer shorts.

Moby

His single art, his dharma, his purpose,
is the reduction of all, a deconstruction
of everything he sees, the long process
of nullity, the issuance of inaction

from action, of nothing from something.
He pursues his stuffed prey, his squeaky toys,
as if they are the dark and sweet stone shining
forth from juicy fruits, only the center of things

will do. He prefers the quietude of dissolution
over absolution. From his solitary perch
on the coarse rock of this volcanic mountain,
Moby sees only the truth buried in the microcosm

of what abides in the discernible world around him—
forget the crows that flap their anger at the sky
uselessly from the fingerless branches of a dead spruce,
forget the dark rain hanging precariously from the high

elbows of an oak tree, forget the dark face of the sky
and the warm soil, forget the rich trembling sound
of the trains running on their rails. He would deny
it all for a length of soft hemp rope any day—or a bone

long buried, a sweet treasure for him to gnaw,
to take apart, to examine with canine teeth
and saliva and claws. He will fuss over it with jaws
hardwired tight with the ancient philosophy of dogs,

and with his sorrowful eyes, view the object of his desire,
a lovely beef bone under his paws—as his own fine shooting star.

Tag

In a city such as this, you steal Kenwood
and Harmon-Kardon stereos from row houses
and from the dashboards of badass tinted
and chromed and lowered hydraulic-injected

turbo rides with even bigger and more badass
owners and dealers and pimps and embezzlers
who all sport hate tattoos on their elbows
or ears or necks or calves or privates or scalps.

So you steal to get the slick acrylic paint
you need to spill your colors and your messages
on the rail cars. The security guards at the rail
yards have guns, so you have made your own

invention to attach to the spray cans—a silencer
made of cardboard tp rolls, duct tape, and a plastic
bucket with a hole cut in the bottom. You tag
with the hard acrylic so that the epistles you send

out to small towns like Flagstaff and Santa Fe
and Barstow and Huntsville and Tallahassee can
be seen for what they are: a shout out into the void
of America, a note in a bottle that rattles on hot rails,

and you hope deep down that someone will see your words,
that they will travel the hard track back into the wild night,
that for once someone will come looking for you without
punishment or violence or retribution on their minds,

and when they arrive, accompanied by the deep echoed wail
of the rail cars and the hot dark breath of swirling prairie dreams,
you hope they will finally carry the message that saves you.

More Things Olivia Brings to the Party

Somewhere along the way
they take it away from
you, the belief that happiness

is a possibility, an absolute, a right,
a truth. Our conviction ticks off slowly
like the whipping of a chronometer

on a piano, our background music
for life pounded out crudely by a child with
a PB&J in one hand and disillusion

in the other. And most of us,
we stumble along to the din
of this cacophony of sound, growing

more and more sure that our
joy is just the tonic to what is
truly important; take for example

my list of necessities from three years ago:
running water, fried tomatoes, flat screen TV,
Heidi Klume, sunroof, lilangel4506 in chat

room PLEASUREDOME, garage door
opener, more publications, more god
(or something like god—that thing

that changes accountability to manifest
destiny, that thing that most of us believe
makes us American), and lastly a comfortable

sofa minus the smell of urine. Somewhere along
the way, the list becomes the pleasure, then
the work for the list becomes the pleasure,

then one day you find yourself pouring
over a receipt at a restaurant, looking
for a way to leave less of a tip—the

difference between fifteen and twenty
percent Huge! At five bucks. It is then,
too late! that you realize that you have lost all

charity, and that this missing god you hope to find
is disappointed in you, and that he dreams
of the day he can match your charity with

his charity. But maybe you will be as lucky
as I am, and he will take pity on you, and
one day, you will be listening to music from Jewel

(I know) as you drive a date home, and you will
look at the girl in the seat next to you,
and you will see what the glory of eternity

looks like when bubblegum, a good wrench set,
a digital CD/alarm clock/ipod, and The List,
dissolve away and reveal the woman you

have been searching for all along, and
if you listen carefully, you will hear a jam band
tuning up in the background, ready to rock
you all the way through the rest of your life.

Acknowledgements:

Grateful acknowledgement is made to the following journals and publications, in which these poems (some in different versions) are forthcoming or have appeared:

River Styx: "Watermelon Truck Near Arabi, GA."
Rosebud: "Dublin."
Pif Magazine and Prose Ax: "The Focus of the Thousand Mile Stare."
Chautauqua: "The Cold Logic of Farm Animals."
Atlanta Review: "Tag," and "More Things Olivia Brings to the Party."
Witness: "Sunshine Running Wild."
Rattle: "Regrets Number 191: The Bosnian."
Antioch Review: "The Karma Suite."
Indiana Review and Camphorweed: "And the Way the Sun Was Positioned."
Slipstream: "Four Cats, an Hundred Roaches, Two Dogs."
Rhino and Meridian: "Alpen Suiss."
Stirring: "How to Look West From Mount Pleasant, Utah."
Southern Poetry Review, Poetry Motel, and *LSR*: "Golem."
River City Review/The Pinch: "Mormon Boy."
The MacGuffin: "And the Way the Sun Was Positioned,"
North American Review and The God Particle: "Falling In Love During Wartime."
Red Owl Review: "Things I Know About Dublin."
American Diaspora: "How to Look West From Mount Pleasant, Utah."
Spoon River Poetry Review: "The Best Man In All the World."
Main Street Rag: "Children and Blind-men and Gods."
Shine Journal and Conceit: "The Road to Baghdad."
Pushcart Prize Nominee 2011.
Reunion: the Dallas Review: "Old Girlfriends Never Die," "How Plastic Feels About the Sun," "Where We Are Going With This," and "Curtain Calls."

I offer my humble and deepest thanks:

To those whom I consider at least partially responsible for the publication of this collection, specifically, Matt Bondurant, Toni Lefton, Jane Springer, and Olivia Eggert; I offer my eternal gratitude. Thank you for believing in me, and for working nearly as hard on this project as I did. Thank you to Dana Curtis and everyone at the Elixir Press, for bringing this manuscript to life.

Special thanks to the Creative Writing and English Programs at the San Francisco State University and the Northern Arizona University, especially Jane Armstrong Woodman, Ann Cummins, Miles Waggoner, and Jim Simmerman, for teaching me it was not enough to want to write. Heartfelt and earnest thanks to the writers, poets, and staff of the English Department at the Florida State University, specifically Mark Winegardner, David Kirby, and Julianna Baggott, who taught me how to be a writer. Your kindnesses number too many to count.

Thanks to Carol Houck Smith for her scholarship, and to Michael Collier, Ellen Bryant Voigt, Jennifer Grotz, Noreen Cargill, R. Dwayne Betts, Richard Bausch, and all the staff, writers, and poets at the Bread Loaf Writer's Conference.

Thank you to the 82nd Airborne Division and all the soldiers who do the work no one else will—you have provided so much fodder for my writing life. To the Salerno and Sicily drop-zones at Fort Bragg, NC; thank you for not killing me. Thanks as well to my earliest mentors, before I realized I had them or needed them: Roger Mork, Carol Born, John McDonald, and all the police officers in Lander, Wyoming, who took pity on me.

Huge thanks to all my friends, too numerous to count, for your love and loyalty and inspiration—I am truly lucky to have you all in my life. Most of all, thank you Mom, thank you Dad, thank you big brothers, and thank you little sister, and thank you to my extended and large Mormon family, most of whom would find this collection distasteful—I am truly sorry for those images I cannot ignore, and for their demand on the profane. I tried to edit out as many of the really bad words as I could. Honestly.

And finally, thank you to Olivia, my wife and true love, who picked me up, rubbed off the grime and grit, hammered out the dents and dings, shined me up, and set me on my path again.

Poetry Titles from Elixir Press

Circassian Girl by Michelle Mitchell-Foust

Imago Mundi by Michelle Mitchell-Foust

Distance From Birth by Tracy Philpot

Original White Animals by Tracy Philpot

Flow Blue by Sarah Kennedy

A Witch's Dictionary by Sarah Kennedy

Monster Zero by Jay Snodgrass

Drag by Duriel E. Harris

Running the Voodoo Down by Jim McGarrah

Assignation at Vanishing Point by Jane Satterfield

The Jewish Fake Book by Sima Rabinowitz

Recital by Samn Stockwell

Murder Ballads by Jake Adam York

Floating Girl (Angel of War) by Robert Randolph

Puritan Spectacle by Robert Strong

Keeping the Tigers Behind Us by Glenn J. Freeman

Bonneville by Jenny Mueller

Cities of Flesh and the Dead by Diann Blakely

The Halo Rule by Teresa Leo

Perpetual Care by Katie Cappello

The Raindrop's Gospel: The Trials of St. Jerome and St. Paula
by Maurya Simon

Prelude to Air from Water by Sandy Florian

Let Me Open You A Swan by Deborah Bogen

Spit by Esther Lee

Rag & Bone by Kathryn Nuernberger

Kingdom of Throat-stuck Luck by George Kalamaras

Mormon Boy by Seth Brady Tucker

Nostalgia for the Criminal Past by Kathleen Winter

Little Oblivion by Susan Allspaw

Fiction titles

How Things Break by Kerala Goodkin
Nine Ten Again by Phil Condon
Memory Sickness by Phong Nguyen

Limited Edition Chapbooks

Juju by Judy Moffat
Grass by Sean Aden Lovelace
X-testaments by Karen Zealand
Rapture by Sarah Kennedy
Green Ink Wings by Sherre Myers
Orange Reminds You Of Listening by Kristin Abraham
In What I Have Done & What I Have Failed To Do by Joseph P. Wood
Hymn of Ash by George Looney
Bray by Paul Gibbons